WILD ABOUT
PIZZA AND PASTA

BY LOIS M. CRISTOFANO

D1370795

BARRON'S

Woodbury, New York • London • Toronto • Sydney

To my husband, Sully, my mother, and of course, Truffles

All inquiries should be addressed to:
Barron's Educational Series, Inc.
113 Crossways Park Drive
Woodbury, New York 11797

Library of Congress No. 85-3889
International Standard Book No. 0-8120-2912-7

Library of Congress Cataloging in Publication Data
Cristofano, Lois
   Wild about pizza and pasta.

   Includes index.
   1. Pizza.   2. Cookery (Macaroni)   I. Title.
TX770.C76   1985   641.8'22   85-3889
ISBN 0-8120-2912-7

Design by Milton Glaser, Inc.
Color photographs by Karen Leeds
Helga Weinrib, food stylist
Linda Peacock, prop stylist

PRINTED IN THE UNITED STATES OF AMERICA

5 6 7 8   510   9 8 7 6 5 4 3 2

CONTENTS

INTRODUCTION

This is a cookbook designed to simplify the mystique of pasta and pizza. All of the ingredients are readily available in your everyday supermarket. We have not included recipes to make your own pasta, but offer you recipes that are old favorites with new twists. The pasta sauces have been developed to inspire you to experiment according to your taste.

Pasta is simple to prepare—no special equipment is needed except a large pot of boiling, salted water.

The pizza recipes are created to include new combinations of familiar ingredients which will combine to give you new flavor associations appealing to the everyday taste as well as the gourmet appetite.

Pasta—what is it? Pasta is the generic term for many varieties of products that are made from flour, water, and sometimes eggs. Pasta made with all-purpose flour into a basic dough makes a fine-textured, very delicate and light product, which lends itself well to ravioli and lasagne. The combination of semolina flour and all-purpose flour yields a product that has real body with a resilient quality. Semolina flour is made from winter wheat, which has a high gluten content. This is why pasta holds its shape when cooked and does not fall apart. The term pasta covers all macaroni and egg noodle products, as well as Oriental noodles.

The question of which pasta with which sauce has as many different answers as there are pasta shapes. The best choice usually is to follow your own creative instincts; but as a general rule, rich, meaty sauces usually go best with short, chunky pasta, such as ziti or rigatoni. Tomato sauces generally go well with long thin pasta shapes which are hollow. Creamy, butter or béchamel-based sauces accompany fine, delicate and small pasta shapes.

All pasta sauces can be served with either fresh or packaged pasta. The main difference between fresh and packaged pasta is the amount of preparation and cooking time required. Freshly prepared pasta, either homemade or purchased, should be used quickly. Fresh pasta cooks in a matter of minutes. It also yields slightly less than the packaged pasta because it has more moisture. Therefore, it absorbs less water when cooking and will swell less than packaged pasta. Packaged pasta is less expensive and easier to store. It keeps well on the pantry shelf and is ready to use when you need it quickly or unexpectedly. You will be wise to purchase fresh or packaged pasta if you lack the time to make your own. Improperly prepared, homemade pasta can be gummy, mushy and may even disintegrate when cooked.

How to cook pasta properly: Pasta can easily be ruined by improper cooking techniques. By following these *simple directions, you will have perfectly cooked pasta every time.*

1. Use a minimum of 4 quarts of water for 1 pound of pasta. Never use less than 3 quarts of water for any amount of pasta, even a small amount. Do not ever cook more than 2 pounds of pasta at the same time in the same pot. It will be difficult to stir and to drain properly.

2. Bring the 4 quarts of water to a rapid boil in a large kettle. When water has reached a full rolling boil, add 1 tablespoon of salt and 1 tablespoon of olive oil. Let water return to a full rolling boil.

3. Add pasta, making sure that all of it is covered by water. Spaghetti or other long strands of packaged pasta may have to be bent, but not broken, to force them below the water surface. Stir pasta frequently.

4. Start testing for doneness about 4 minutes into cooking. Pasta must be cooked al dente or just until tender, but firm. Drain immediately. Transfer to a warm bowl or platter and toss with prepared sauce. It is of the utmost importance that the cooked pasta is quickly tossed with the sauce to prevent it from sticking together and becoming a gummy mass. Serve immediately. It is interesting to note that Italians like a little sauce on their pasta, whereas most Americans prefer a larger amount. As a general rule, use

1 cup sauce for 4 ounces of dry pasta and you'll please most palates.

Packaged pasta is generally classified as long and narrow, short and broad, flat or tubular, solid or hollow and smooth-ridged. Each shape has a name. Here are the best known names:

Bucatini: *also known as perciatelli. Thick, hollow spaghetti.*

Conchiglie: *means seashells. With ridges they are called cocciglie rigate.*

Farfelle: *means butterflies.*

Fusilli: *corkscrew-shaped spaghetti. Also known as tortiglioni or rotelle.*

Lumache: *means snails.*

Linguini: *flat and long like noodles and slightly tapered at the edges.*

Maccheroncini: *are small short, hollow macaroni. If ridged, it is called rigati.*

Pastinina: *covers many miniature pastas such as ditalini, acini, mezzanellini.*

Penne: *means pens, feathers or quills. They are shaped like a quill and are cut diagonally at both ends.*

Rigatoni: *is short, hollow and slightly curved.*

Spaghetti and spaghettini: *thin noodles. In Southern Italy it is called vermicelli and vermicellini.*

Tortellini: *means little twisted one.*

Ziti: *are short, smooth and narrow tubular shapes.*

Today, pizza is no longer just for kids or for a snack. It is one of the most simple dishes to prepare right in your own kitchen. Just follow these easy guidelines.

When assembling your pizzas, remember to leave a 1-inch rim of dough around the outer edge to prevent leakage. To prevent the bottom pizza crust from becoming undercooked and soggy, just fill the center of the pie with a minimum of ingredients, because as the pie bakes the cheeses and sauces will melt and run to the center of the baked pizza. Baked pizzas are easier to serve when removed from their baking pan to a wooden board and cut with a pizza wheel or scissors.

If time is limited, it is possible to freeze unbaked pizza crusts directly on pan. Remove frozen crusts from pan; wrap securely in freezer bag and store in freezer for up to 4 months. It is possible to shape pizza dough after it has been kneaded and before it has risen by shaping it into a flat disk. Wrap securely in plastic wrap or freezer bag and keep in the freezer for up to 4 months. When ready to use, defrost in refrigerator for 24 hours; then let stand in a warm place for 1 hour; roll and stretch pizza dough to fit pan and top with any QUICKIE TOPPING:

1. Keep several good-quality, ready-made pizza sauces on your pantry shelf. To vary the flavor of prepared sauce, simmer for 10 minutes with a little sautéed chopped onion and garlic. Add additional seasoning such as leaf basil or oregano and red pepper flakes.

2. For quick pizza garnish, use bottled artichoke hearts, canned tuna, canned sardines, green or black olives, canned anchovy fillets, dry salami and bottled roasted red peppers.

3. Spread thick pizza sauce over loaf of halved French bread. Top with grated mozzarella and other garnishes. Broil just until cheese is melted and bubbly.

CONVERSION TABLES

The weights and measures in the lists of ingredients and cooking instructions for each recipe are in both U.S. and metric units.

LIQUID MEASURES

The Imperial cup is considerably larger than the U.S. cup. Use the following table to convert to Imperial liquid units.

AMERICAN CUP (in book)	IMPERIAL CUP (adjusts to)
¼ cup	4 tablespoons
⅓ cup	5 tablespoons
½ cup	8 tablespoons
⅔ cup	¼ pint
¾ cup	¼ pint + 2 tablespoons
1 cup	¼ pint + 6 tablespoons
1¼ cups	½ pint
1½ cups	½ pint + 4 tablespoons
2 cups	¾ pint
2½ cups	1 pint
3 cups	1½ pints
4 cups	1½ pints + 4 tablespoons
5 cups	2 pints

Note: The Australian and Canadian cup measures 250 mL and is only slightly larger than the U.S. cup, which is 236 mL. Cooks in Australia and Canada can follow the exact measurements given in the recipes, using either the U.S. or metric measures.

SOLID MEASURES

British and Australian cooks measure more items by weight. Here are approximate equivalents for basic items in the book.

	U.S. Customary	Imperial
Butter	1 tablespoon	½ oz.
	¼ cup	2 oz.
	½ cup	4 oz.
	1 cup	8 oz.
Cheese (grated)	½ cup	2 oz.
Flour, all-purpose (sifted)	¼ cup	1¼ oz.
	1 cup	5 oz.
Herbs (fresh, chopped)	¼ cup	¼ oz.
Meats (chopped)	1 cup	6-8 oz.
Nuts (chopped)	¼ cup	1 oz.
	1 cup	4 oz.
Vegetables (chopped, such as onions, carrots)	½ cup	2 oz.
	1 cup	4 oz.

OVEN TEMPERATURES

British cooks should use the following settings.

Gas Mark	¼	2	4	6	8
Fahrenheit	225	300	350	400	450
Celsius	110	150	180	200	230

A NOTE ABOUT INGREDIENTS

The names for ingredients used in this book are terms that will be familiar to U.S. and Canadian cooks. For cooks in England and Australia, be aware of the following:

All-purpose flour = Plain flour
Heavy cream = Double cream
Light cream = Single cream
Eggplant = Aubergine
Prosciutto = Parma ham
Tomato paste = Tomato concentrate
Zucchini = Courgette or small marrow

PASTA APPETIZERS

CHEESE AND PROSCIUTTO STUFFED ROLLS

MAKES 36

INGREDIENTS

1 medium onion, chopped
1 clove garlic, peeled and chopped
2 tablespoons olive oil
1 can (28 ounces/800 g) Italian-style tomatoes
1 can (6 ounces/175 g) tomato paste
1 teaspoon leaf basil, crumbled
1 teaspoon salt
½ cup (125 mL) water
½ pound (225 g) ricotta cheese
½ pound (225 g) Fontina cheese, shredded
¼ cup (30 g) freshly grated Parmesan cheese
¼ pound (115 g) prosciutto, finely chopped
2 teaspoons chopped fresh basil, or 1 teaspoon leaf basil, crumbled
1 egg yolk
½ teaspoon salt
¼ teaspoon pepper
12 lasagna noodles

Sauté onion and garlic in oil in medium saucepan until tender; stir in tomatoes, tomato paste, basil, salt, and water; blend well.

Bring to boiling; lower heat and simmer uncovered, stirring frequently, for 30 minutes, or until sauce has thickened. Cool to room temperature. Set aside.

Combine ricotta, Fontina, Parmesan, chopped prosciutto, basil, egg yolk, salt, and pepper in large bowl; blend well.

Cook lasagna noodles in boiling, salted water until al dente or just until tender, but firm. Drain. Wipe dry with cloth towel (do not use paper toweling; it will stick to cooked noodle).

Opposite: Cheese and Prosciutto Stuffed Rolls

Spread prepared cheese filling evenly onto cooked noodles. Roll each lasagna noodle firmly and securely. Place seam side down in a single layer in large shallow dish. Cover with plastic wrap. Chill for at least 1 hour.

To serve, gently cut each roll into thirds. Serve with prepared tomato sauce, which has been reheated.

TUNA-STUFFED SHELLS WITH ANCHOVY DIP

MAKES 60

INGREDIENTS

4 cloves garlic, peeled and chopped
4 tablespoons (60 g) butter
¼ cup (35 g) all-purpose flour
1 cup (240 mL) milk
1 cup (240 mL) heavy cream
½ cup (15 g) finely chopped
fresh parsley
6 flat anchovy fillets, drained
and finely chopped
½ teaspoon salt
¼ teaspoon pepper
½ pound (225 g) ricotta cheese
½ pound (225 g) small-curd
cottage cheese
¼ cup (30 g) freshly grated
Parmesan cheese
1 can (7 ounces/200 g) tuna,
drained and flaked
¼ cup (7 g) chopped fresh parsley
2 tablespoons finely chopped
drained capers
1 teaspoon lemon juice
2 egg yolks, well beaten
1 package (12 ounces/340 g)
large pasta shells

Sauté garlic in butter in medium saucepan just until it starts to turn golden brown, about 3 minutes. Stir in flour; stir constantly for about 2 minutes. Remove from heat. Stir in milk and heavy cream; blend well.

Cook, stirring constantly, until sauce thickens and bubbles, about 3 minutes. Stir in parsley, chopped anchovies, salt, and pepper; blend well. Set aside.

Combine ricotta, cottage cheese, Parmesan, tuna, parsley, capers, lemon juice, and egg yolks in large bowl; mix well. Preheat oven to 300°F (150°C).

Cook pasta shells in boiling, salted water until al dente or just until tender, but firm. Drain. Stuff each shell with cheese mixture, pressing it down lightly to fill out the shell shape. Press opening of shell together lightly so that the shape of the shell remains. Place stuffed shells in large shallow baking dish in single layer. Place in oven for 10 minutes to heat thoroughly.

To serve, use wooden picks to skewer stuffed shells and dip in hot anchovy dip.

TORTELLINI WITH GORGONZOLA-WALNUT DIP

MAKES ABOUT 125

INGREDIENTS

¼ pound (115 g) Gorgonzola cheese, crumbled
⅓ cup (75 mL) milk
3 tablespoons (45 g) butter
¼ cup (60 mL) heavy cream
⅓ cup (40 g) freshly grated Parmesan cheese
⅓ cup (40 g) chopped walnuts
1 quart (950 mL) chicken broth
1 pound (450 g) fresh or frozen cheese-filled tortellini

Combine Gorgonzola, milk, butter, heavy cream, and Parmesan cheese in medium skillet. Cook over medium heat, stirring frequently until cheeses have melted and mixture turns creamy. Keep warm over low heat, stirring frequently while cooking tortellini. Add walnuts to skillet mixture.

Bring chicken broth to boiling in a large pot. Add tortellini; return to boiling. Cook for 5 to 7 minutes or until al dente. Drain.

To serve, use wooden picks to skewer tortellini and dip into hot Gorgonzola dip.

PASTA SOUPS

ESCAROLE AND ORZO SOUP

SERVES 4

INGREDIENTS

1 head of escarole, about ¾ to
1 pound (450 g)
2 tablespoons finely chopped onion
¼ cup (60 g) butter
½ teaspoon salt
3½ cups (825 mL) beef broth
½ cup (125 g) orzo
(rice-shaped pasta)
3 tablespoons freshly grated
Parmesan cheese

Remove outer leaves of escarole; trim and wash thoroughly. Cut into ½ inch (1½ cm) wide pieces.

Sauté onion in butter in a large kettle over medium heat until golden brown, about 3 minutes. Add escarole; sauté for 1 minute, stirring frequently.

Add salt and ½ cup (125 mL) broth. Cover; cook over very low heat until escarole is tender, about 30 minutes.

Add remaining broth. Cover. Bring to boiling; add orzo. Cook over medium heat just until orzo is tender, about 10 minutes, stirring frequently. Remove from heat. Stir in Parmesan cheese.

Note

If fresh escarole is unavailable, substitute fresh spinach or 2 packages (10 ounces/285 g each) frozen chopped spinach, thawed and drained.

Pour boiling water over beans to cover in large kettle; let stand 1 hour. Drain.

Combine beans with 1 quart (950 mL) water in large, heavy kettle. Cook over medium heat just until almost tender, about 35 minutes. Add broth and crushed tomatoes; cook for 10 minutes.

Sauté salt pork, bacon, or pork chops in medium skillet over medium heat until browned. Add onion, celery, carrot, and garlic. Cook for 3 to 5 minutes. Stir in flour and 1 cup (240 mL) of hot bean liquid until smooth; add to beans. Stir in pepper and macaroni. Cover; simmer until beans and macaroni are tender, about 10 minutes. Sprinkle with parsley and grated Parmesan cheese.

PASTA E FAGIOLI

SERVES 6

INGREDIENTS

1 cup (225 g) dried navy beans
1 quart (950 mL) water
6 cups (1¼ L) beef broth
1 cup (240 mL) Italian tomatoes, crushed
½ cup (115 g) chopped salt pork, bacon or 2 small boned pork chops
1 medium onion, chopped
1 stalk celery, chopped
1 medium carrot, chopped
1 clove garlic, peeled and chopped
1 tablespoon all-purpose flour
½ teaspoon pepper
1 cup (225 g) small, tubular macaroni or ditalini
⅓ cup (10 g) chopped fresh parsley
½ cup (60 g) freshly grated Parmesan cheese

23

MINESTRONE SOUP

SERVES 4

INGREDIENTS

3 tablespoons olive oil
1 medium onion, chopped
2 stalks celery, chopped
1 clove garlic, peeled and chopped
1 teaspoon chopped fresh rosemary,
or ½ teaspoon leaf rosemary,
crumbled
2 carrots, peeled and sliced
1 can (16 ounces/450 g)
tomatoes, crushed
1 package (10 ounces/285 g)
frozen peas
1 can (16 ounces/450 g) white
kidney beans
2 cans (13¾ ounces/390 g each) beef
broth, about 3½ cups (825 mL)
¼ cup (60 g) ditalini or other
small pasta
2 tablespoons chopped fresh parsley
½ cup (60 g) freshly grated
Parmesan cheese

Heat oil in large saucepan; sauté onion, celery, and garlic until tender, about 5 minutes.

Add rosemary and vegetables; cook over medium heat for 5 minutes to blend flavors; add broth. Bring to boiling; lower heat, simmer 20 minutes.

Add pasta; cook 10 more minutes or until pasta is al dente.

Combine parsley and cheese; serve with minestrone.

PASTA SALADS

EGG, SALMON, AND SHELL SALAD

SERVES 8

INGREDIENTS

1 package (16 ounces/450 g)
small pasta shells

1 can (16 ounces/450 g) red salmon,
drained and flaked

4 stalks celery, chopped

4 hard-cooked eggs, peeled
and sliced

½ cup sliced pitted black olives

¼ cup drained capers

1 cup olive oil

1 teaspoon grated lemon rind

2 tablespoons lemon juice

2 tablespoons white wine vinegar

2 tablespoons chopped fresh dill,
or 1 teaspoon dried dillweed

½ teaspoon dry mustard

½ teaspoon salt

¼ teaspoon pepper

Crisp lettuce leaves

Cook pasta shells in boiling, salted water until al dente or just until tender, but firm. Drain. Cool slightly.

Combine cooked shells, salmon, celery, eggs, olives, and capers in large bowl; toss gently to mix well.

Combine olive oil, lemon rind, lemon juice, vinegar, dill, mustard, salt, and pepper in a small jar with a tight-fitting lid; cover and shake well. Pour over salad; toss gently.

Turn salad into lettuce-lined bowl. Chill before serving.

Wash eggplant; pierce skin in several places with a fork. Bake in a moderate oven (350°F/180°C) for 45 minutes or until tender. Cool.

Peel eggplant; cut pulp into ½-inch (1½-cm) dice. Combine eggplant, onion, chopped tomatoes, sliced mushrooms, chopped green pepper, and sliced zucchini in a large bowl; toss to mix well.

Combine garlic, olive oil, lemon juice, vinegar, parsley, oregano, salt, and pepper in a small jar with a tight-fitting lid; cover and shake well. Pour over eggplant mixture.

Cook ziti in boiling, salted water until al dente or just until tender, but firm. Drain.

Toss cooked ziti with eggplant mixture; mix well. Cover with plastic wrap. Chill in refrigerator for several hours to blend flavors. Serve at room temperature.

ZITI VEGETABLE SALAD WITH EGGPLANT DRESSING

SERVES 8

INGREDIENTS

1 large eggplant, 1½ to 2 pounds (600 to 900 g)

1 large onion, chopped

2 large tomatoes, chopped

1 pound (450 g) medium mushrooms, sliced

1 large green pepper, chopped

2 medium zucchini, thinly sliced

2 cloves garlic, peeled and chopped

1 cup (240 mL) olive oil

2 tablespoons lemon juice

2 tablespoons red wine vinegar

⅓ cup (10 g) chopped fresh parsley

2 teaspoons chopped fresh oregano, or 1 teaspoon leaf oregano, crumbled

2 teaspoons salt

½ teaspoon pepper

1 package (16 ounces/450 g) ziti

HERRING AND PASTA SALAD WITH CURRIED CREAM DRESSING

SERVES 6

INGREDIENTS

8 ounces (225 g) rotelle

2 medium cucumbers, peeled, seeded and chopped

6 pickled herring fillets in wine sauce, drained and cut into ½-inch (1½-cm) pieces

¼ cup (60 mL) wine vinegar

¼ cup (60 mL) olive oil

½ teaspoon salt

2 cups (450 mL) dairy sour cream

1½ tablespoons curry powder

8 green onions, chopped

Cook rotelle in boiling, salted water until al dente or just until tender, but firm. Drain.

Combine cooked rotelle, chopped cucumber, and herring in large bowl; toss to mix well.

Combine vinegar, oil, and salt in small bowl; whisk until smooth. Pour over herring mixture. Cover with plastic wrap. Chill at least 2 hours.

Blend sour cream and curry powder together in small bowl until well blended. Stir into marinated pasta salad. Sprinkle with chopped green onions.

Cook ditali in boiling, salted water until al dente or just until tender, but firm. Drain. Cool slightly.

Cook chicken breasts in water or chicken broth to cover in large saucepan for 30 minutes. Cool. Skin, bone and cut meat into thin slices.

Combine cooked pasta, chicken, Boston and romaine lettuces, celery, and crumbled bacon in large salad bowl; toss gently to mix well.

Halve avocado; peel and pit. Cut into cubes; sprinkle with lemon juice.

Add tomatoes, eggs, avocado, and Gorgonzola cheese to salad bowl. Combine oil, vinegar, mustard, salt, pepper and basil in jar with a tight-fitting lid; cover and shake well. Pour over salad and toss gently to mix well.

CHEF'S PASTA SALAD

SERVES 8

INGREDIENTS

1 package (16 ounces/450 g) ditali or other short tubular pasta
2 whole chicken breasts, about 12 ounces (340 g) each
1 small head Boston lettuce, broken into bite-size pieces
1 small head romaine lettuce, broken into bite-size pieces
1 cup (115 g) sliced celery
6 slices bacon, cooked and crumbled
1 ripe avocado
1 tablespoon lemon juice
2 ripe tomatoes, cut into thin wedges
4 hard-cooked eggs, peeled and sliced
¼ pound (115 g) Gorgonzola cheese, crumbled
¾ cup (175 mL) olive oil
½ cup (125 mL) tarragon vinegar
2 teaspoons dry mustard
¾ teaspoon salt
¼ teaspoon pepper
1 teaspoon chopped fresh basil, or ½ teaspoon leaf basil, crumbled

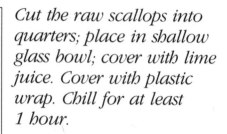

SEVICHE GAZPACHO SALAD

SERVES 12

INGREDIENTS

1 pound (450 g) sea scallops
⅔ cup (150 mL) lime juice
⅓ cup (10 g) chopped fresh parsley
¼ cup (30 g) chopped onion
¼ cup (30 g) chopped green pepper
6 tablespoons (85 mL) olive oil
½ teaspoon salt
¼ teaspoon pepper
1 can (46 ounces/1⅓ L) tomato juice
1 medium onion, chopped
1 red or green pepper, seeded and chopped
1 jalapeño pepper, seeded and chopped
½ cup (15 g) chopped fresh cilantro
or parsley
3 cloves garlic, peeled and chopped
4 medium tomatoes, peeled,
seeded and chopped
⅓ cup (75 mL) olive oil
⅓ cup (75 mL) lime juice
⅓ cup (75 mL) red wine vinegar
½ teaspoon salt
¼ teaspoon pepper
1 package (16 ounces/450 g) penne
or other small pasta

Cut the raw scallops into quarters; place in shallow glass bowl; cover with lime juice. Cover with plastic wrap. Chill for at least 1 hour.

Drain. Add parsley, onion, green pepper, olive oil, salt, and pepper. Cover. Chill.

Combine tomato juice, onion, peppers, cilantro, garlic, tomatoes, olive oil, lime juice, vinegar, salt, and pepper in large bowl; mix well. Cover with plastic wrap. Chill several hours or overnight.

To serve, cook penne in boiling, salted water until al dente or just until tender, but firm. Drain. Cool slightly. Combine with chilled gazpacho and scallop mixture; toss gently to mix well. Chill 1 hour.

Cook butterflies or bowties in boiling, salted water until al dente or just until tender, but firm. Drain. Cool slightly.

Combine oil, vinegar, garlic, mustard, basil, parsley, and chives in a jar with a tight-fitting lid. Cover. Shake well. Pour half over cooked pasta, onions, and green beans in large bowl.

Line salad bowl with lettuce leaves. Turn pasta into bowl. Arrange tuna fish, tomato wedges, sardines, egg halves, anchovy fillets, and olives over pasta. Pour remaining dressing over all.

PASTA SALAD NIÇOISE

SERVES 8

INGREDIENTS

1 package (16 ounces/450 g) butterflies or bowties
1 cup (240 mL) olive oil
¼ cup (60 mL) red wine vinegar
2 cloves garlic, peeled and chopped
1 teaspoon dry mustard
2 teaspoons chopped fresh basil, or 1 teaspoon leaf basil, crumbled
2 tablespoons chopped fresh parsley
2 teaspoons chopped chives
6 green onions, chopped
1 package (10 ounces/285 g) frozen cut green beans, thawed
1 small head Boston lettuce, separated into leaves
2 cans (7 ounces/200 g each) tuna fish, drained and flaked
3 large ripe tomatoes, cut into wedges
2 cans (4 ounces/115 g each) sardines, drained
6 hard-cooked eggs, peeled and halved
1 can (2 ounces/60 g) anchovy fillets, drained
½ cup (60 g) pitted black olives, halved

31

Opposite: Pasta Salad Niçoise (p. 31)

PASTA WITH SEAFOOD

RED CLAM SAUCE WITH SPAGHETTINI

SERVES 4

INGREDIENTS

1 large onion, chopped
4 cloves garlic, peeled and chopped
¼ cup (60 mL) olive oil
2 cans (8 ounces/225 g each) minced clams
6 ripe medium tomatoes, peeled and coarsely chopped; or
1 can (28 ounces/800 g) Italian plum tomatoes, crushed
1 can (2 ounces/60 g) anchovy fillets, drained
1 teaspoon salt
1 teaspoon chopped fresh basil, or ½ teaspoon leaf basil, crumbled
1 teaspoon chopped fresh oregano, or ½ teaspoon leaf oregano, crumbled
½ teaspoon pepper
2 tablespoons chopped fresh parsley
1 package (16 ounces/450 g) spaghettini

Sauté onion and garlic in oil in medium saucepan until tender, about 5 minutes. Drain liquid from clams into saucepan, reserving clams. Add tomatoes, anchovy fillets, salt, basil, oregano, and pepper. Bring to boiling; lower heat. Simmer uncovered, 15 minutes, stirring frequently, until sauce is thickened. Stir in reserved clams and parsley. Heat for 5 minutes or until clams are thoroughly heated.

Cook spaghettini in boiling, salted water until al dente or just until tender, but firm. Drain. Toss with clam sauce.

Scrub mussels well; cover with cold water and vinegar. Let soak for 4 hours.

Cut shrimp down the back lengthwise with kitchen shears, being careful not to cut all the way through. Wash and pat dry.

Melt butter with oil in large skillet over medium heat. Sauté garlic just until lightly golden brown.

Add mussels and shrimp; sauté, stirring constantly, 5 to 6 minutes or just until shrimp turns pink and mussels open. Add parsley and lemon.

Cook linguini in boiling, salted water until al dente or just until tender, but firm. Drain. Toss with shrimp and mussel sauce.

WHITE SHRIMP-MUSSEL SAUCE WITH LINGUINI

SERVES 6

INGREDIENTS

2 dozen fresh mussels
1 tablespoon white vinegar
1 pound (450 g) medium shrimp, peeled and deveined
½ cup (115 g) butter
½ cup (125 mL) olive oil
3 cloves garlic, peeled and chopped
2 tablespoons chopped fresh parsley
1 lemon, cut into thin slices
1 package (16 ounces/450 g) linguini

TUNA AND RICOTTA MANICOTTI WITH CHEESE SAUCE

SERVES 6

INGREDIENTS

12 manicotti shells
1 can (7 ounces/200 g) tuna, drained and flaked
1 cup (240 mL) ricotta cheese, sieved
1 cup (240 mL) heavy cream
2 cups (225 g) freshly grated Parmesan cheese
½ teaspoon salt
¼ teaspoon pepper

Cook the manicotti shells in boiling, salted water until al dente or just until tender, but firm. Drain. Preheat oven to 400°F (200°C).

Combine tuna and ricotta until smooth. Using a pastry bag fitted with a plain tube, filled with tuna mixture, pipe mixture into cooked manicotti shells.

Combine heavy cream, Parmesan, salt, and pepper; blend well. Spoon a small amount of cheese sauce into the bottom of a buttered 13 × 9 × 2-inch (30 × 25 × 5-cm) baking pan. Line filled manicotti shells in buttered pan. Pour remaining cheese sauce over manicotti.

Bake for 25 to 30 minutes until hot and golden brown.

Cook cauliflower and broccoli flowerettes in boiling water to cover in large saucepan just until tender, about 7 to 8 minutes. Drain.

Cook anchovy fillets in oil in skillet over medium heat until they become a paste. Add drained vegetables, pepper, and butter; toss lightly. Cook over medium heat for 5 minutes.

Cook capellini in boiling, salted water until al dente or just until tender, but firm. Drain.

Toss pasta with anchovy/vegetable sauce until mixed. Sprinkle with grated Parmesan and Romano cheeses.

CAPELLINI WITH CAULIFLOWER, BROCCOLI, AND ANCHOVY SAUCE

SERVES 4

INGREDIENTS

1 cup (115 g) fresh cauliflower flowerettes
1 cup (115 g) fresh broccoli flowerettes
8 medium flat anchovy fillets, drained and chopped
6 tablespoons (85 mL) olive oil
½ teaspoon pepper
1 tablespoon (15 g) butter
1 package (16 ounces/450 g) capellini or other thin long spaghetti
6 tablespoons (40 g) freshly grated Parmesan cheese
6 tablespoons (40 g) freshly grated Romano cheese

SMOKED SALMON WITH FUSILLI IN CREAMY CHEESE SAUCE

SERVES 4

INGREDIENTS

8 ounces (225 g) thinly sliced
smoked salmon, chopped
⅓ cup (75 g) butter
¼ cup (60 mL) brandy
1⅓ cups (315 mL) heavy cream
1 package (16 ounces/450 g) fusilli
1 cup (115 g) freshly grated
Parmesan cheese
½ teaspoon pepper
2 teaspoons chopped fresh dill,
or 1 teaspoon dillweed
¼ cup (7 g) chopped fresh parsley

Sauté salmon in butter in large skillet over medium heat until salmon becomes pale pink, about 3 minutes. Add brandy; ignite brandy and let alcohol burn off.

Add heavy cream. Cook over medium heat until cream is thoroughly heated.

Cook fusilli in boiling, salted water until al dente or just until tender, but firm. Drain. Pour salmon mixture over pasta; sprinkle Parmesan, pepper, dillweed, and parsley over salmon. Toss gently to mix well.

Wash and pat shrimp dry. Sprinkle with lemon juice.

Sauté green onions and garlic in oil in a large skillet until tender, about 3 minutes. Stir in chopped tomatoes, wine, basil, 1 tablespoon of the parsley, salt, and pepper. Lower heat; simmer uncovered, 15 minutes, or until mixture thickens slightly.

Stir in shrimp and lemon juice. Cook over medium heat just until shrimp turns pink and feels firm, about 5 minutes. Remove from heat. Add cheese. Sprinkle with remaining parsley.

Cook mostaccioli in boiling, salted water until al dente or just until tender, but firm. Drain. Toss with shrimp-cheese mixture.

SHRIMP AND FETA CHEESE WITH MOSTACCIOLI À LA GRECQUE

SERVES 8

INGREDIENTS

1½ pounds (680 g) medium shrimp, peeled and deveined
2 tablespoons lemon juice
6 green onions, chopped
1 clove garlic, peeled and chopped
2 tablespoons olive oil
4 small ripe tomatoes, peeled and chopped
½ cup (125 mL) dry white wine
2 teaspoons chopped fresh basil, or 1 teaspoon leaf basil, crumbled
2 tablespoons chopped fresh parsley
1 teaspoon salt
¼ teaspoon pepper
¾ cup (85 g) cubed feta cheese
1 package (16 ounces/450 g) mostaccioli or other short pasta

Opposite: Shrimp and Feta Cheese with Mostaccoili
à la Grecque (p. 39)

PASTA WITH MEAT

TORTELLINI WITH CREAMY MUSHROOM SAUCE

SERVES 6

INGREDIENTS

2 quarts (1¾ L) chicken broth
2 pounds (900 g) fresh or frozen
meat tortellini
2 cups (450 mL) heavy cream
½ pound (225 g) mushrooms, sliced
½ cup (115 g) butter
½ pound (225 g) prosciutto
or ham, diced
1 teaspoon salt
¼ teaspoon Tabasco sauce
¼ teaspoon pepper
⅔ cup (80 g) freshly grated
Parmesan cheese

Bring chicken broth to boiling in large kettle. Add tortellini; cook for 5 to 7 minutes or until almost tender. Drain.

Bring cream to boiling in medium saucepan; add cooked tortellini. Cook uncovered over medium heat for 5 minutes or until tortellini are tender.

Sauté mushrooms in butter in medium skillet over medium heat just until browned. Add prosciutto or ham; cook 3 minutes. Stir into tortellini along with salt, Tabasco, pepper, and Parmesan cheese.

Combine beef, pork or veal, onion, Parmesan, garlic, parsley, basil, egg, and bread crumbs in medium bowl; mix well. Shape into 2-inch (5-cm) balls.

Brown meatballs, a few at a time, in 2 tablespoons olive oil in a large skillet; remove to a large pan.

Sprinkle ½ teaspoon salt over cubed eggplant in colander. Place heavy plate on top of eggplant. Let drain for 30 minutes.

Heat ¼ cup (60 mL) oil in a large skillet; sauté chopped garlic, tomatoes, basil, pepper flakes, and remaining ½ teaspoon salt over medium heat for 15 minutes.

Pat eggplant cubes dry with paper toweling. Heat remaining oil in a separate skillet. Sauté eggplant cubes until browned. Remove with slotted spoon to pan with meatballs. Add tomato sauce. Cook over medium heat just until heated thoroughly.

Cook spaghetti in boiling, salted water until al dente or just until tender, but firm. Drain. Toss gently with meatball-eggplant-tomato sauce. Serve with grated Parmesan, if desired.

SPAGHETTI WITH MEATBALLS AND EGGPLANT

SERVES 6

INGREDIENTS

½ pound (225 g) lean ground beef
½ pound (225 g) lean ground pork or veal
½ cup (60 g) chopped onion
½ cup (60 g) freshly grated Parmesan cheese
1 clove garlic, peeled and chopped
¼ cup (7 g) chopped fresh parsley
1 teaspoon chopped fresh basil, or
½ teaspoon leaf basil, crumbled
1 egg
1 cup (60 g) dry bread crumbs
⅔ cup (150 mL) olive oil
1 teaspoon salt
1 eggplant, about 1 pound (450 g),
peeled and cubed
2 cloves garlic, peeled and chopped
1 can (35 ounces/1 kg) Italian
plum tomatoes, crushed
2 teaspoons chopped fresh basil, or
1 teaspoon leaf basil, crumbled
½ teaspoon dried red pepper flakes
1 package (16 ounces/450 g) spaghetti

BAKED ZITI RAGU BOLOGNESE

SERVES 8

INGREDIENTS

2 carrots, peeled and chopped
2 stalks celery, chopped
2 medium onions, peeled
and chopped
2 cloves garlic, peeled
and chopped
¼ cup (7 g) chopped fresh parsley
¼ cup (60 mL) olive oil
¾ pound (340 g) ground beef chuck
¼ pound (115 g) ground pork
6 tablespoons (75 g) butter
1 can (28 ounces/800 g) Italian
tomatoes, drained and puréed
½ teaspoon salt
¼ teaspoon pepper
2 tablespoons dry white wine
1 teaspoon sugar
1 package (16 ounces/450 g) ziti

Sauté chopped carrot, celery, onion, garlic, and parsley in oil in large saucepan until tender. Add meat. Cook meat, breaking up with a wooden spoon until well browned.

Add butter, tomatoes, salt, pepper, and wine. Simmer for 1 hour. Add sugar; simmer for 30 additional minutes. Preheat the oven to 350°F (180°C).

Cook ziti in boiling, salted water until al dente or just until tender, but firm. Drain. Toss with sauce.

Spread ziti into buttered 3-quart (3-L) baking dish. Bake for 30 to 45 minutes.

Cook artichoke hearts according to package directions. Drain.

Sauté green onions and carrots in butter in a large skillet over medium heat just until tender, about 5 minutes.

Add ham, artichoke hearts, and cream; stir to blend well. Cook over medium heat, stirring frequently until thoroughly heated. Add cheese and parsley.

Cook spaghetti in boiling, salted water until al dente or just until tender, but firm. Drain. Toss with sauce.

SPAGHETTI WITH ARTICHOKE HEARTS, CARROTS AND HAM

SERVES 6

INGREDIENTS

2 packages (9 ounces/250 g)
frozen artichoke hearts
8 green onions, chopped
4 carrots, peeled and diced
¼ cup (60 g) butter
½ pound (225 g) ham, diced
1 cup (240 mL) heavy cream
½ cup (60 g) freshly grated
Parmesan cheese
¼ cup (7 g) chopped fresh parsley
1 package (16 ounces/450 g)
spaghetti

LASAGNA WITH SAUSAGE MEAT SAUCE

SERVES 8

INGREDIENTS

¼ cup olive oil
2 cloves garlic, peeled and chopped
2 large onions, chopped
½ pound (225 g) sweet Italian sausage
½ pound (225 g) hot Italian sausage
1 can (35 ounces/1 kg) Italian plum tomatoes,
crushed
1 can (6 ounces/175 g) tomato paste
2 teaspoons salt
1 teaspoon sugar
2 teaspoons chopped fresh oregano, or
1 teaspoon leaf oregano, crumbled
1 teaspoon chopped fresh basil, or
½ teaspoon leaf basil, crumbled
¼ teaspoon dried red pepper flakes
½ cup (125 mL) water
1 pound (450 g) ground beef
1 egg
1 clove garlic, peeled and chopped
½ teaspoon salt
¼ teaspoon pepper
1 teaspoon chopped fresh basil, or
½ teaspoon leaf basil, crumbled
⅓ cup (10 g) chopped fresh parsley
1 package (16 ounces/450 g) spinach
lasagna noodles
1 pound (450 g) ricotta cheese
½ pound (225 g) mozzarella cheese,
thinly sliced
½ cup (60 g) freshly grated Parmesan cheese

Heat oil in large saucepan; add garlic and onions and sauté over low heat for 10 minutes. Cut sausages into ½-inch (1½-cm) thick pieces. Cook sausages until browned on both sides. Add tomatoes, tomato paste, salt, basil, sugar, oregano, red pepper flakes, and water. Cover; cook over low heat for 1½ hours or until thickened, stirring occasionally.

Combine beef, egg, garlic, salt, pepper, basil, and 2 tablespoons parsley in large bowl. Drop by spoonfuls into fat or oil in large skillet; brown lightly, breaking up with a wooden spoon. Remove to tomato sauce with a slotted spoon. Cook for 30 minutes. Preheat oven to 375°F (190°C).

Cook spinach lasagna noodles in boiling, salted water until al dente or just until tender, but firm. Drain.

Spoon small amount of sauce in bottom of 13 × 9 × 2-inch (30 × 25 × 5-cm) baking pan. Arrange single layer of lasagna in pan, overlapping slightly. Spoon about one-quarter meat sauce over noodles, then one-third ricotta; top with one-quarter mozzarella, grated Parmesan, and a sprinkling of parsley. Repeat layers until all ingredients are used, ending with top layer of sauce and mozzarella.

Bake for 45 minutes or until hot and bubbly.

STRAW AND HAY PASTA WITH HAM

SERVES 8

INGREDIENTS

1 pound (450 g) mushrooms, sliced
¼ cup (30 g) chopped onion
6 tablespoons (75 g) butter
½ teaspooon salt
¼ teaspoon pepper
½ pound (225 g) baked ham,
cut into julienne strips
¾ cup (175 mL) heavy cream
8 ounces (225 g) fettuccine
8 ounces (225 g) spinach fettuccine
1½ pounds (680 g) fresh peas,
shelled, or 1 package (10 ounces/
280 g) frozen peas, thawed
½ cup (60 g) freshly grated
Parmesan cheese

Sauté mushrooms and onion in 3 tablespoons (45 g) butter in large skillet until golden brown. Add salt, pepper, and ham; stir constantly for 1 minute. Add half of the heavy cream; cook just until cream thickens slightly. Remove from heat. Cook fresh peas, covered with 1-inch (2½-cm) boiling water for 8 minutes, or just until tender.

Cook fettuccine in boiling, salted water until al dente or just until tender, but firm. Drain. Cook spinach fettuccine separately in boiling, salted water until al dente or just until tender, but firm. Drain.

Toss cooked pastas and peas with remaining heavy cream and butter. Add half of the mushroom-ham sauce; mix well. Add grated cheese; blend well. Pour in remaining mushroom-ham sauce; cook over medium heat just until pasta and sauce is heated thoroughly. Serve with additional grated Parmesan, if desired.

48

Opposite: Lasagna with Sausage Meat Sauce (p. 46)

PASTA WITH POULTRY

SPINACH, MUSHROOMS, AND CHICKEN IN CHEESE SAUCE

SERVES 6

INGREDIENTS

1 pound (450 g) fresh spinach leaves, cleaned, stemmed, and shredded
½ pound (225 g) mushrooms, sliced
2 tablespoons lemon juice
¼ cup (60 g) butter
1 clove garlic, peeled and chopped
2 tablespoons dry white wine
1 cup (240 mL) heavy cream
2 cups (450 g) diced, cooked chicken
½ teaspoon salt
¼ teaspoon pepper
½ cup (60 g) freshly grated Parmesan cheese
1 package (16 ounces/450 g) thin spaghetti

Cook spinach in boiling, salted water until it is tender, about 5 minutes. Drain very well.

Sprinkle mushrooms with lemon juice. Melt butter in a large skillet; add garlic and mushrooms and sauté until light golden brown. Add wine; simmer for 5 minutes. Add cream; bring mixture to boiling, stirring until well blended. Remove from heat. Stir in diced chicken, salt, pepper, and Parmesan.

Cook spaghetti in boiling, salted water until al dente or just until tender, but firm. Drain. Add drained spinach and mushroom mixture. Toss gently to mix well. Serve with additional grated Parmesan cheese, if desired.

Combine tomatoes, onion, and carrot in medium saucepan. Bring to boiling, breaking up tomatoes with wooden spoon. Lower heat; simmer uncovered, 15 minutes. Purée mixture, a small amount at a time, in container of electric blender or food processor.

Sauté garlic in oil in large saucepan for 1 minute. Stir in puréed tomato mixture, basil, salt, red pepper flakes, parsley, and diced chicken. Cook 5 minutes.

Cook spaghetti in boiling, salted water until al dente or just until tender, but firm. Drain. Toss with prepared chicken-marinara sauce.

CHICKEN CACCIATORE WITH PASTA

SERVES 4

INGREDIENTS

1 can (35 ounces/1 kg) Italian plum tomatoes
1 large onion, chopped
1 large carrot, peeled and chopped
2 cloves garlic, peeled and chopped
¼ cup (60 mL) olive oil
2 teaspoons chopped fresh basil, or 1 teaspoon leaf basil, crumbled
½ teaspoon salt
¼ teaspoon dried red pepper flakes
¼ cup (7 g) chopped fresh parsley
2 cups (450 g) diced, cooked chicken
1 package (16 ounces/450 g) spaghetti

TURKEY SPINACH TETRAZZINI

SERVES 16

INGREDIENTS

1 cup (225 g) butter
½ cup (70 g) all-purpose flour
4 cups (950 mL) chicken broth
2 cups (450 mL) heavy cream
1 cup (240 mL) dry white wine
¼ teaspoon pepper
⅛ teaspoon ground nutmeg
½ pound (225 g) Swiss cheese,
shredded
1 pound (450 g) medium
mushrooms, thinly sliced
2 packages (16 ounces/450 g each)
linguini
2 packages (10 ounces/285 g each)
frozen chopped spinach, thawed
3 cups (675 g) diced, cooked turkey
1¼ cups (85 g) fresh bread crumbs
⅓ cup (75 g) butter, melted
⅓ cup (40 g) freshly grated
Parmesan cheese
¼ cup (7 g) chopped fresh parsley

Melt ½ cup (115 g) butter in large saucepan; blend in flour. Cook, stirring constantly, 1 minute. Gradually stir in chicken broth, heavy cream, and wine. Cook, stirring constantly, until sauce thickens and bubbles. Add pepper and nutmeg. Continue to cook 1 minute. Remove from heat. Stir in shredded cheese until melted. Set aside.

Sauté mushrooms in remaining butter in a large skillet just until golden brown. Set aside.

Cook linguini in boiling, salted water until al dente or just until tender, but firm. Drain. Turn into a well-buttered 5-quart (5-L) shallow baking dish. Preheat oven to 350°F (180°C).

Press excess liquid from thawed spinach. Add mushrooms, spinach, and turkey pieces to linguini; mix well. Pour cheese sauce over linguini; toss gently to mix well.

Combine bread crumbs, melted butter, Parmesan, and chopped parsley in a small bowl; mix well. Sprinkle over dish evenly.

Bake for 30 minutes or until bubbly and lightly browned.

CHICKEN PRIMAVERA WITH LINGUINI

SERVES 6

INGREDIENTS

1 bunch broccoli, about 1 pound (450 g)
2 small zucchini
½ pound (225 g) asparagus
1 package (16 ounces/450 g) linguini
1 large clove garlic, peeled and chopped
1 pint (450 g) cherry tomatoes,
stemmed and halved
¼ cup (60 mL) olive oil
2 teaspoons chopped fresh basil, or
1 teaspoon leaf basil, crumbled
½ pound (225 g) mushrooms, thinly sliced
1½ pounds (680 g) fresh peas, shelled and
blanched 8 minutes, or 1 package
(10 ounces/285 g) frozen peas
¼ cup (7 g) chopped fresh parsley
1½ teaspoons salt
¼ teaspoon pepper
¼ teaspoon red pepper flakes
2 cups (450 g) diced, cooked chicken
¼ cup (60 g) butter
1 cup (240 mL) heavy cream
⅔ cup (80 g) freshly grated Parmesan cheese

Wash and trim broccoli, zucchini, and asparagus. Cut broccoli into bite-size pieces; cut zucchini into thin slices; cut asparagus into 1-inch (2½-cm) pieces. Cook in boiling, salted water until crisp-tender, about 5 minutes; drain. Place in large bowl.

Cook linguini in boiling, salted water until al dente or just until tender, but firm. Drain.

Sauté garlic and tomatoes in oil in large skillet for 2 minutes. Stir in basil and mushrooms; cook for 3 minutes. Stir in peas, parsley, salt, pepper, red pepper flakes, and diced chicken. Cook 1 minute more. Add mixture to vegetables in bowl.

Melt butter in same skillet; stir in cream and cheese. Cook over medium heat, stirring constantly, just until smooth. Add linguini, toss to coat well. Stir in vegetables; heat gently just until thoroughly hot.

Cook bacon and garlic in large skillet until browned. Add chicken. Heat for 3 minutes. Set aside.

Cook spaghetti in boiling, salted walter until al dente or just until tender, but firm. Drain. Add to skillet; stir gently, just until well coated. Remove from heat. Set aside.

Beat egg yolks in a small bowl with a wire whisk or fork until well blended, light and fluffy. Add cream, 1/3 cup (40 g) Parmesan cheese, and pepper.

Pour egg mixture over the spaghetti. Stir quickly to coat well. Serve with remaining grated Parmesan, if desired.

CHICKEN CARBONARA

SERVES 4

INGREDIENTS

1 clove garlic, peeled and chopped
1/4 pound (115 g) bacon, diced
1 cup (225 g) diced, cooked chicken
1 package (16 ounces/450 g)
spaghetti
4 egg yolks
2 tablespoons heavy cream
2/3 cup (80 g) freshly grated
Parmesan cheese
1/4 teaspoon black pepper

Opposite: Creamy Cheese Pasta Primavera (p. 62)

PASTA WITH VEGETABLES AND CHEESE

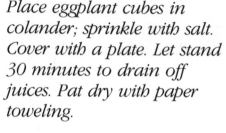

RATATOUILLE LASAGNA

SERVES 8

INGREDIENTS

1 eggplant, about 1 pound (450 g),
peeled and cubed
½ teaspoon salt
4 medium onions, thinly sliced
4 medium green peppers, cut into
½-inch (1½-cm) chunks
½ cup (125 mL) olive oil
3 small zucchini, sliced
½ pound (225 g) mushrooms, sliced
1 can (35 ounces/1 kg) Italian
plum tomatoes, crushed
½ cup (15 g) chopped fresh parsley
1 can (6 ounces/175 g) tomato paste
1 bay leaf
2 teaspoons chopped fresh thyme, or
1 teaspoon leaf thyme, crumbled
1 package (14 ounces/400 g)
lasagna noodles
1 pound (450 g) mozzarella cheese,
shredded
1 cup (115 g) freshly grated
Parmesan cheese

Place eggplant cubes in colander; sprinkle with salt. Cover with a plate. Let stand 30 minutes to drain off juices. Pat dry with paper toweling.

Sauté onions and green peppers in ¼ cup (60 mL) olive oil in large skillet over medium heat until tender, about 15 minutes. Stir in eggplant cubes, zucchini, and mushrooms; sauté just until tender.

Add tomatoes, parsley, tomato paste, bay leaf, and thyme; simmer over medium heat, stirring frequently for about 30 minutes.

Cook lasagna noodles in boiling, salted water until al dente or just until tender, but firm. Drain. Preheat oven to 350°F (180°C).

Spoon small amount of ratatouille in bottom of 13 × 9 × 2-inch (30 × 25 × 5-cm) baking pan. Arrange single layer of lasagna noodles in pan, overlapping slightly. Spoon one-quarter of ratatouille, one-quarter mozzarella cheese, and all of Parmesan cheese over noodles. Repeat layers until all ingredients are used, ending with top layer of sauce and mozzarella.

Bake for 45 minutes, or until hot and bubbly.

SPINACH PESTO LASAGNA

SERVES 8

INGREDIENTS

4 cloves garlic, peeled and crushed

⅔ cup (70 g) pine nuts

4 to 6 tablespoons chopped fresh basil, or 2 to 3 tablespoons leaf basil, crumbled

2 cups (115 g) fresh spinach leaves, washed well and chopped; or 2 cups (60 g) loosely packed parsley sprigs

1½ cups (350 mL) olive oil

1¾ cups (200 g) freshly grated Parmesan cheese

1 package (16 ounces/450 g) lasagna noodles

1 pound (450 g) ricotta cheese

1 pound (450 g) mozzarella cheese, shredded

Purée garlic, nuts, basil, and spinach or parsley with ½ cup (125 mL) oil in an electric blender or food processor at low speed. Pour purée into a bowl; gradually stir in remaining oil, a little at a time, beating well after each addition.

Stir in ¾ cup (85 g) grated Parmesan cheese; let stand to let flavors blend. Preheat oven to moderate, 350°F (180°C).

Cook lasagna noodles in boiling, salted water until al dente or just until tender, but firm. Drain.

Spoon a small amount of pesto sauce into an ungreased 13 × 9 × 2-inch (30 × 25 × 5-cm) baking pan. Arrange a single layer of cooked lasagna noodles, overlapping slightly. Spread a

small amount of pesto sauce, ricotta and mozzarella and remaining cup of Parmesan over noodles evenly.

Repeat layers until all ingredients are used, ending with ricotta and mozzarella.

Bake uncovered for 35 to 45 minutes until lightly browned and bubbly. Let stand 10 minutes before cutting.

Serve with additional grated Parmesan cheese, if desired.

CREAMY CHEESE PASTA PRIMAVERA

SERVES 8

INGREDIENTS

1½ cups (175 g) broccoli flowerettes
1 pound (450 g) fresh snow peas; or
1 package (10 ounces/285 g)
frozen peas, thawed
3 medium zucchini, sliced
3 medium yellow squash, sliced
¼ cup (125 mL) olive oil
2 cloves garlic, peeled and chopped
½ pound (450 g) mushrooms, sliced
1 pint (450 g) cherry tomatoes,
stemmed and halved
½ cup (15 g) chopped fresh parsley
½ cup (60 g) pine nuts
1 package (16 ounces/450 g)
spaghetti
⅓ cup (75 g) butter
½ cup (60 g) freshly grated
Parmesan cheese
1 cup (125 mL) heavy cream
2 tablespoons chopped fresh basil, or
1 tablespoon leaf basil, crumbled

Blanch broccoli, snow peas, zucchini, and yellow squash separately in boiling, salted water to cover, in medium saucepan for 1 to 2 minutes. Drain.

Heat 1 tablespoon oil in large skillet; sauté garlic and mushrooms just until lightly browned, about 3 minutes. Add cherry tomatoes, parsley, and pine nuts; cook over medium heat for 3 minutes. Remove from heat. Set aside.

Cook spaghetti in boiling, salted water until al dente or just until tender, but firm. Drain.

Melt butter in large kettle; add Parmesan cheese, heavy cream, and basil. Cook over medium heat, stirring constantly until cheese melts and sauce becomes creamy.

Add vegetables to cheese sauce, toss gently. Spoon over cooked spaghetti. Serve with additional grated Parmesan cheese, if desired.

Combine walnuts, olive oil, Parmesan cheese, parsley, onion, garlic, basil, oregano, salt, and pepper in container of electric blender. Cover. Whirl until smooth.

Blanch zucchini in boiling, salted water to cover for 3 minutes. Drain. Add to container of electric blender; cover, whirl until smooth.

Cook pasta in boiling, salted water until al dente or just until tender, but firm. Drain.

Place sauce in medium saucepan. Cook over medium heat just until heated through. Pour over pasta; toss to mix well. Serve with additional grated Parmesan cheese, if desired.

ZUCCHINI AND WALNUT SAUCE FOR PASTA

SERVES 4

INGREDIENTS

2 cups (225 g) toasted walnuts
1 cup (240 mL) olive oil
½ cup (60 g) freshly grated
Parmesan cheese
¼ cup (115 g) chopped fresh parsley
¼ cup (30 g) chopped onion
1 clove garlic, peeled and chopped
2 teaspoons chopped fresh basil, or
1 teaspoon leaf basil, crumbled
2 teaspoons chopped fresh oregano,
or 1 teaspoon leaf oregano, crumbled
½ teaspoon salt
¼ teaspoon pepper
2 medium zucchini, sliced
1 package (16 ounces/450 g)
tagliatelle or other flat pasta

LINGUINI WITH MUSHROOMS, PEAS, FOUR-CHEESE SAUCE

SERVES 6

INGREDIENTS

1½ pounds (680 g) fresh peas, shelled, or 1 package (10 ounces/ 285 g) frozen peas, thawed

½ cup (115 g) butter

½ pound (225 g) mushrooms, sliced

4 ounces (115 g) Muenster or fontina cheese, cubed

4 ounces (115 g) Gorgonzola cheese, cubed

4 ounces (115 g) mozzarella cheese, cubed

1 package (16 ounces/450 g) spinach linguini

1 cup (115 g) freshly grated Parmesan cheese

1 cup (240 mL) heavy cream

Cook fresh peas, covered in 1-inch (2½-cm) boiling water for 8 minutes, or just until tender.

Melt 4 tablespoons (60 g) butter in large skillet; sauté peas and mushrooms just until lightly browned. Add remaining butter, Muenster or fontina, Gorgonzola, and mozzarella cheeses. Cook over low heat, stirring constantly until cheeses melt. Note: Mixture may become stringy. Keep warm over very low heat.

Cook pasta in boiling, salted water until al dente or just until tender, but firm. Drain.

Add Parmesan cheese to sauce; stir over low heat until melted. Stir in cream. Cook over low heat, stirring constantly until cream is well blended with cheeses. Do not boil the sauce.

Toss pasta with sauce until well mixed.

Opposite: Artichoke Heart & Anchovy Pizza (p. 75)

Sauté zucchini in olive oil in medium skillet until light, golden brown. Let drain on paper toweling.

Cook fusilli in boiling, salted water until al dente or just until tender, but firm. Drain.

Melt butter and olive oil in large skillet. Dissolve flour in milk. Stir into hot butter. Add sautéed zucchini, salt, and basil. Cook over medium heat for 3 minutes, stirring constantly. Remove from heat.

Quickly stir in egg yolk and grated Parmesan cheese; mix well. Pour sauce over cooked fusilli; toss gently to mix well. Serve with additional grated Parmesan cheese, if desired.

FUSILLI WITH CREAMY ZUCCHINI AND BASIL SAUCE

SERVES 4

INGREDIENTS

1 pound (450 g) zucchini, cut into julienne strips
½ cup (125 mL) olive oil
1 package (16 ounces/450 g) fusilli
3 tablespoons (45 g) butter
3 tablespoons olive oil
1 teaspoon all-purpose flour
⅓ cup (75 mL) milk
½ teaspoon salt
2 tablespoons chopped fresh basil, or 1 tablespoon leaf basil, crumbled
1 egg yolk
¾ cup (85 g) freshly grated Parmesan cheese

PIZZAS

HOMEMADE PIZZA DOUGH

MAKES ONE 18-INCH (45-cm) CRUST

INGREDIENTS

1 level teaspoon active dry yeast
1 cup (240 mL) very warm water
(110° to 115°F)
3 to 3½ cups (450 g)
all-purpose flour
½ teaspoon salt

Sprinkle yeast over very warm water in a large bowl. Stir gently with a fork until yeast is dissolved and liquid becomes light brown. Add 1 cup (150 g) flour and salt; mix thoroughly with a wooden spoon. Add second cup flour; mix until dough begins to form a soft sticky mass.

Scrape dough out onto floured board. Knead third cup of flour or more if needed into dough, a little at a time, until no longer sticky. Continue to knead just until smooth and elastic, about 5 to 10 minutes.

Place dough in lightly oiled 2-quart (2-L) bowl; turn to coat with oil. Tightly cover bowl with plastic wrap. Let rise in warm place away from drafts until doubled in bulk, about 30 to 45 minutes.

After dough has risen, punch down. Turn out onto board. Knead 1 minute. Cover with a clean towel. Let rest 15 minutes.

Combine tomatoes, basil, garlic, tomato paste, salt, and pepper in heavy 2-quart (2-L), non-aluminum saucepan. Crush tomatoes with wooden spoon.

Bring to boiling, stirring frequently. Lower heat; simmer uncovered, 45 to 60 minutes, stirring frequently until sauce thickens. Cool.

THICK PIZZA SAUCE

MAKES 4 CUPS (950 mL)

INGREDIENTS

1 can (35 ounces/1 kg) Italian plum tomatoes in purée or juice

2 teaspoons chopped fresh basil, or 1 teaspoon leaf basil, crumbled

1 clove garlic, peeled and chopped

2 tablespoons tomato paste (optional)

½ teaspoon salt

¼ teaspoon pepper

NEW YORK–STYLE PIZZA

MAKES ONE 18-INCH (45-cm) PIZZA

INGREDIENTS

1 recipe Homemade Pizza Dough (pg. 68)

½ pound (225 g) mushrooms, chopped

1 tablespoon olive oil

½ pound (225 g) mozzarella cheese, cut into ¼-inch (¾-cm) thick slices

2 large cloves garlic, peeled and finely chopped

½ pound (225 g) sweet Italian sausage, removed from casings and crumbled

½ pound (225 g) pepperoni, thinly sliced

1 cup Thick Pizza Sauce (pg. 69)

2 teaspoons chopped fresh oregano, or 1 teaspoon leaf oregano, crumbled

¼ cup (30 g) freshly grated Parmesan cheese

1 tablespoon olive oil

Preheat oven to very hot, 450°F (230°C). Grease an 18-inch (45-cm) pizza pan; sprinkle with cornmeal. Roll and stretch Homemade Pizza Dough to fit pan.

Sauté chopped mushrooms in 1 tablespoon olive oil in medium skillet until golden brown.

Quickly assemble toppings to prevent dough from getting soggy in the following order: sliced mozzarella, garlic, crumbled sausage, sautéed mushrooms, and pepperoni. Spoon Thick Pizza Sauce evenly over top. Sprinkle with oregano and Parmesan cheese. Drizzle with 1 tablespoon olive oil.

Bake for 5 to 10 minutes or until golden brown and crusty.

Preheat oven to very hot, 500°F (280°C). Lightly oil a 16-inch (40-cm) pizza pan; sprinkle with cornmeal.

Roll and stretch Homemade Pizza Dough to fit pan.

Sauté onion in 1 tablespoon oil in medium skillet until soft, but not brown. Remove to bowl. Sauté zucchini slices in remaining 1 tablespoon oil in same skillet, stirring frequently for 3 minutes. Remove to bowl.

Cook sausage in same skillet in boiling water to cover for 10 minutes. Remove from skillet; cool. Cut into thin slices.

Spread Thick Pizza Sauce evenly over crust. Sprinkle with three-fourths of the mozzarella and all of the Parmesan. Arrange zucchini, sausage, and onion over cheese; sprinkle with remaining mozzarella.

Bake for 15 minutes or until lightly browned.

SAUSAGE AND ZUCCHINI PIZZA

MAKES ONE 16-INCH (40-cm) PIZZA

INGREDIENTS

1 recipe Homemade Pizza Dough (pg. 68)
1 large onion, thinly sliced
2 tablespoons olive oil
1 pound (450 g) zucchini, thinly sliced
1 pound (450 g) sweet Italian sausage
2 cups (450 mL) Thick Pizza Sauce (pg. 69)
1 pound (450 g) mozzarella cheese, shredded
½ cup (60 g) freshly grated Parmesan cheese

DEEP-DISH PIZZA

**MAKES ONE 15 × 10-INCH
(38 × 25-cm) PIZZA**

INGREDIENTS

2 recipes Homemade Pizza Dough
(pg. 68)
1 cup Thick Pizza Sauce (pg. 69)
⅓ cup (40 g) freshly grated
Parmesan cheese
1 large green pepper, halved, seeded
and cut into strips
1 large red pepper, halved, seeded
and cut into strips
1 large onion, thinly sliced
½ pound (225 g) mushrooms,
thinly sliced
½ pound (225 g) pepperoni,
thinly sliced
1 package (8 ounces/225 g)
mozzarella cheese, shredded
2 teaspoons chopped fresh oregano,
or 1 teaspoon leaf oregano, crumbled
1 tablespoon olive oil

*Preheat oven to 450°F
(230°C). Lightly oil a 15 ×
10 × 1-inch (38 × 25 ×
5-cm) jelly roll pan; sprinkle
with cornmeal. Roll and
stretch Homemade Pizza
Dough to fit pan, making
sure that dough is up to the
edge of pan to form a rim.*

*Spread Thick Pizza Sauce
evenly over crust; sprinkle
with grated Parmesan.*

*Arrange sliced green and red
pepper strips, onions,
mushrooms, and pepperoni
over top; sprinkle with
shredded mozzarella cheese.
Sprinkle with oregano and
drizzle with olive oil.*

*Bake 15 to 20 minutes or
until crust is golden brown
and cheese is melted and
bubbly.*

Opposite: Deep-Dish Pizza

Preheat oven to very hot, 500°F (280°C). Lightly oil an 18-inch (45-cm) pizza pan; sprinkle with cornmeal.

Roll and stretch Homemade Pizza Dough to fit pan.

Place mozzarella over crust, then sprinkle with garlic and prosciutto; pour Thick Pizza Sauce over. Sprinkle with basil, Parmesan, and parsley. Drizzle with olive oil.

Bake for 10 minutes or until golden brown and crusty.

PROSCIUTTO AND MOZZARELLA CHEESE

MAKES ONE 18-INCH (45-cm) PIZZA

INGREDIENTS

1 recipe Homemade Pizza Dough (pg. 68)

½ pound (225 g) mozzarella cheese, cut into ¼-inch (¾-cm) thick slices

1 large clove garlic, peeled and chopped

½ pound (225 g) prosciutto, finely shredded

1 cup Thick Pizza Sauce (pg. 69)

2 teaspoons chopped fresh basil, or 1 teaspoon leaf basil, crumbled

¼ cup (30 g) freshly grated Parmesan cheese

¼ cup (7 g) chopped fresh parsley

1 tablespoon olive oil

PIZZA PRIMAVERA

MAKES ONE 18-INCH (45-cm) PIZZA

INGREDIENTS

1 recipe Homemade Pizza Dough (pg. 68)
1 cup Thick Pizza Sauce (pg. 69)
1 large fresh ripe tomato, sliced
1 large clove garlic, peeled and finely chopped
1 large green pepper, halved, seeded and cut into strips
1 large red pepper, halved, seeded and cut into strips
1 package (10 ounces/285 g) frozen artichoke hearts, thawed, drained and halved
½ pound (225 g) mushrooms, sliced
1 cup (115 g) shredded fontina cheese
1 cup (115 g) shredded mozzarella cheese
½ cup (60 g) freshly grated Parmesan cheese
2 teaspoons chopped fresh basil, or 1 teaspoon leaf basil, crumbled
1 tablespoon olive oil

Preheat oven to very hot, 500°F (280°C). Lightly oil an 18-inch (45-cm) pizza pan; sprinkle with cornmeal.

Roll and stretch Homemade Pizza Dough to fit pan.

Spread Thick Pizza Sauce over crust. Arrange tomato slices, garlic, green and red pepper strips, artichoke hearts, and mushrooms over sauce. Sprinkle with shredded fontina, mozzarella, and grated Parmesan. Sprinkle with basil. Drizzle with olive oil.

Bake 15 minutes or until cheeses have melted and pizza is golden brown.

*Preheat oven to very hot,
500°F (280°C). Lightly oil an
18-inch (45-cm) pizza pan;
sprinkle with cornmeal.*

*Roll and stretch Homemade
Pizza Dough to fit pan.*

*Spread Thick Pizza Sauce
over crust. Arrange flaked
tuna, olives, mushrooms and
artichoke hearts over sauce.
Sprinkle with shredded
mozzarella cheese.*

*Bake for 15 minutes or until
crust is golden. Garnish with
anchovies.*

ARTICHOKE HEART AND ANCHOVY PIZZA

**MAKES ONE 18-INCH (45-cm)
PIZZA**

INGREDIENTS

1 recipe Homemade Pizza Dough
(pg. 68)

1½ cups (350 mL) Thick Pizza Sauce
(pg. 69)

1 can (7 ounces/200 g) tuna fish,
drained and flaked

1 cup (115 g) pitted black olives,
sliced

½ pound (225 g) mushrooms, sliced

2 jars (4 ounces/115 g each)
marinated artichoke hearts, drained

½ pound (225 g) mozzarella cheese,
shredded

2 cans (2 ounces/60 g each)
rolled anchovies

SPINACH PIZZA

MAKES ONE 18-INCH (45-cm) PIZZA

INGREDIENTS

1 recipe Homemade Pizza Dough
(pg. 68)
2 packages (10 ounces/280 g each)
frozen chopped spinach,
thawed and drained
2 medium onions, thinly sliced
3 tablespoons (45 g) butter
¼ teaspoon ground nutmeg
⅛ teaspoon ground cloves
⅛ teaspoon cayenne pepper
½ cup (125 mL) dairy sour cream
1 egg
8 ounces (225 g) Swiss cheese,
shredded
¼ cup (30 g) freshly grated
Parmesan cheese

Preheat oven to very hot, 500°F (280°C). Lightly oil an 18-inch (45-cm) pizza pan; sprinkle with cornmeal.

Roll and stretch Homemade Pizza Dough to fit pan.

Place spinach in colander; squeeze as much liquid as possible out.

Sauté onions in butter in large skillet until lightly browned. Remove about ¼ cup (60 g); reserve. Combine spinach, nutmeg, cloves, and cayenne into onions in skillet. Cook, stirring frequently until almost all of the liquid evaporates. Cool slightly.

Combine sour cream and egg in medium bowl until blended. Stir in cooled spinach mixture, 1½ cups (175 g) of shredded Swiss cheese and grated Parmesan cheese; blend well. Spread evenly over crust. Sprinkle with remaining shredded Swiss cheese.

Bake for 10 minutes or until cheese is melted and crust is golden. Garnish with reserved sautéed onions.

Preheat oven to very hot, 500°F (280°C). Lightly oil an 18-inch (45-cm) pizza pan; sprinkle with cornmeal. Roll and stretch Homemade Pizza Dough to fit pan.

Sauté mushrooms in olive oil in small skillet just until golden brown. Set aside.

Sprinkle shredded mozzarella over crust; then spread Thick Pizza Sauce over cheese. Arrange chicken, garlic, onion and oregano over sauce. Sprinkle Parmesan over all. Drizzle with 1 tablespoon oil.

Bake for 10 to 15 minutes or until crust is golden.

CHICKEN MARINARA PIZZA

MAKES ONE 18-INCH (45-cm) PIZZA

INGREDIENTS

1 recipe Homemade Pizza Dough (pg. 68)

½ pound (225 g) mushrooms, thinly sliced

1 tablespoon olive oil

½ pound (225 g) mozzarella cheese, shredded

1 cup (240 mL) Thick Pizza Sauce (pg. 69)

1 cup (225 g) chopped, cooked chicken

3 cloves garlic, peeled and finely chopped

1 small onion, finely chopped

2 teaspoons chopped fresh oregano, or 1 teaspoon leaf oregano, crumbled

¼ cup (30 g) freshly grated Parmesan cheese

1 tablespoon olive oil

SAUSAGE AND PEPPERS PIZZA

MAKES ONE 14-INCH (35-cm) PIZZA

INGREDIENTS

1 recipe Homemade Pizza Dough (pg. 68)

½ pound (225 g) sweet Italian sausage

1 can (15 ounces/425 g) tomato sauce

1 green pepper, halved, seeded and cut into strips

1 red pepper, halved, seeded and cut into strips

2 small onions, thinly sliced

8 ounces (225 g) mozzarella cheese, shredded

¼ cup (30 g) freshly grated Parmesan cheese

Preheat oven to very hot, 450°F (230°C). Lightly oil a 14-inch (35-cm) pizza pan. Sprinkle with cornmeal. Roll and stretch Homemade Pizza Dough to fit pan.

Remove sausage from casings; sauté meat in large skillet until no longer pink. Add tomato sauce; cook, stirring frequently, until juices have evaporated and mixture is thickened, about 5 minutes. Remove from heat; cool slightly. Spread meat mixture over dough.

Bake for 10 minutes; remove from oven. Arrange peppers and onions over top; sprinkle with mozzarella and Parmesan cheeses. Return to oven. Bake 15 to 20 minutes longer or until crust is golden brown and cheeses have melted.

Preheat oven to very hot, 450°F (230°C). Grease an 18-inch (45-cm) pizza pan; sprinkle with cornmeal. Roll and stretch Homemade Pizza Dough to fit pan.

Bake for 5 minutes. Remove from oven; leave oven on.

Combine oil, vinegar and mustard in bowl until blended. Brush two-thirds of mixture over partially baked crust, leaving ½-inch (1½-cm) border. Arrange ham and cheese slices over top. Brush with remaining oil mixture.

Bake for 10 to 15 minutes or until cheese has melted and crust is lightly browned.

HAM AND CHEESE PIZZA

MAKES ONE 18-INCH (45-cm) PIZZA

INGREDIENTS

1 recipe Homemade Pizza Dough (pg. 68)
1 tablespoon vegetable oil
1 tablespoon red wine vinegar
2 teaspoons Dijon-style mustard
½ pound (225 g) thinly sliced baked ham
½ pound (225 g) thinly sliced Swiss or Muenster cheese

PIZZA RUSTICA

MAKES ONE 12-INCH (30-cm) DOUBLE CRUST PIZZA

INGREDIENTS

1 recipe Homemade Pizza Dough (pg. 68)

1 container (15 ounces/425 g) ricotta cheese

8 ounces (225 g) shredded mozzarella or pizza cheese

¼ pound (115 g) salami, finely diced

⅓ cup (40 g) sliced green onion

3 tablespoons chopped fresh parsley

2 teaspoons chopped fresh oregano, or 1 teaspoon leaf oregano, crumbled

1 teaspoon salt

3 eggs, slightly beaten

Preheat oven to moderate, 350°F (180°C).

Combine ricotta, mozzarella, or pizza cheese, salami, green onion, parsley, oregano, salt, and eggs, reserving about 2 tablespoons of the beaten egg for brushing.

Punch dough down and divide in half. Lightly oil a 12-inch (30-cm) pizza pan. Stretch one half of Homemade Pizza Dough to fit pan, pressing dough against side of pan to make an edge. Brush edge with reserved beaten egg. Spoon filling over dough. Roll remaining half of dough to a 12-inch round; fit over filling, pressing edge together. Prick entire surface with a 2-tined fork. Cut decorations from trimmings. Brush top with egg. Decorate top. Brush decorations.

Bake for 50 minutes or until golden brown. Cover top with foil if pizza is browning too fast. Let stand 15 minutes before cutting into wedges to serve.

Opposite: Pizza Rustica

Preheat oven to very hot, 450°F (230°C). Grease an 18-inch (45-cm) pizza pan; sprinkle with cornmeal. Roll and stretch Homemade Pizza Dough to fit pan.

Sprinkle 1 cup (115 g) shredded mozzarella over dough; then sprinkle shredded fontina, Parmesan, and crumbled Gorgonzola over mozzarella. Sprinkle parsley, basil, and oregano over Gorgonzola. Top with remaining mozzarella.

Bake for 15 minutes or until cheeses have melted.

FOUR-CHEESE PIZZA

MAKES ONE 18-INCH (45-cm) PIZZA

INGREDIENTS

1 recipe Homemade Pizza Dough (pg. 68)

2 cups (225 g) shredded mozzarella cheese

1 cup (115 g) shredded fontina cheese

1 cup (115 g) freshly grated Parmesan cheese

¼ pound (115 g) Gorgonzola cheese, crumbled

¼ cup (7 g) chopped fresh parsley

2 teaspoons chopped fresh basil, or 1 teaspoon leaf basil, crumbled

1 teaspoon chopped fresh oregano, or ½ teaspoon leaf oregano, crumbled

PIZZA WITH SMOKED SALMON AND CAVIAR

MAKES ONE 18-INCH (45-cm) PIZZA

INGREDIENTS

1 recipe Homemade Pizza Dough (pg. 68)

¼ cup (60 mL) olive oil

1 package (8 ounces/225 g) whipped cream cheese, softened

4 ounces (115 g) smoked salmon, cut into thin strips

¼ cup (7 g) finely chopped chives

⅓ cup (40 g) American golden caviar or salmon roe caviar

Preheat oven to very hot, 450°F (230°C). Grease an 18-inch (45-cm) pizza pan; sprinkle with cornmeal. Roll and stretch Homemade Pizza Dough to fit pan.

Brush dough with olive oil. Bake for 10 minutes or until golden brown and puffed.

Remove pizza from oven; spread top with softened cream cheese. Top pizza with salmon, chives, and caviar.

Preheat oven to very hot, 450°F (230°C). Grease an 18-inch (45-cm) pizza pan; sprinkle with cornmeal. Roll and stretch Homemade Pizza Dough to fit pan.

Combine parsley sprigs, pine nuts, ¼ cup (30 g) grated Parmesan, garlic, basil, and ½ cup (125 mL) olive oil in container of electric blender or food processor. Cover. Process until mixture is well blended.

Sauté mushrooms in remaining oil in medium skillet over medium heat just until golden brown.

Spread pizza dough with pesto sauce. Arrange mushrooms on top. Sprinkle with remaining Parmesan and mozzarella. Sprinkle with chopped green onions.

Bake for 15 to 20 minutes or until cheeses have melted and crust is lightly brown.

SPINACH PESTO AND MUSHROOM PIZZA

MAKES ONE 18-INCH (45-cm) PIZZA

INGREDIENTS

1 recipe Homemade Pizza Dough (pg. 68)
2 cups (60 g) loosely packed parsley sprigs
¼ cup (30 g) pine nuts
½ cup (60 g) freshly grated Parmesan cheese
2 cloves garlic, peeled
2 tablespoons chopped fresh basil, or 1 tablespoon leaf basil, crumbled
¾ cup (175 mL) olive oil
½ pound (225 g) mushrooms, thinly sliced
2 cups (225 g) shredded mozzarella cheese
6 green onions, thinly sliced

GOAT CHEESE PIZZA

MAKES ONE 18-INCH PIZZA

INGREDIENTS

1 recipe Homemade Pizza Dough
(pg. 68)
1 pound (450 g) mozzarella cheese,
thinly sliced
¼ pound (115 g) prosciutto, chopped
1 cup (115 g) crumbled goat cheese
¼ teaspoon chopped fresh parsley
2 teaspoons chopped fresh basil, or
1 teaspoon leaf basil, crumbled

Preheat oven to very hot, 450°F (230°C). Grease an 18-inch (45-cm) pizza pan; sprinkle with cornmeal. Roll and stretch Homemade Pizza Dough to fit pan.

Arrange mozzarella slices over dough. Sprinkle prosciutto and crumbled cheese evenly over mozzarella.

Combine parsley and basil; sprinkle over cheese.

Bake for 15 minutes or until cheeses have melted.

INDEX

FAVORITE RECIPES

_____

_____

_____

_____

_____

_____

_____

_____

_____

_____

_____

_____

_____

FAVORITE RECIPES

FAVORITE RECIPES

_____

_____

_____

_____

_____

_____

_____

_____

_____

_____

_____

_____

FAVORITE RECIPES

FAVORITE RECIPES

FAVORITE RECIPES

FAVORITE RECIPES

FAVORITE RECIPES

FAVORITE RECIPES

Lois Cristofano is a leading food writer and editor, with over 20 years experience. Her articles have appeared regularly in Family Circle *magazine, and she runs a catering business in Bridgehampton, New York.*